e qui es aux cieux!

om soit sanctifié;

gne vienne;

onté soit faite sur la terre comme a

us aujourd'hui notre pain quotidien;

nous nos offenses,

us aussi nous pardonnons à ceux qui nous ont offensés;

duis pas en tentation,

re-nous du malin.

toi qu'appartiennent, dans tous les siècles,

a puissance et la gloire.

h

ukaitu u nahnia.

koba?a tomoba?atu nakwu waitusu.

hu tuhkarui.

katu. Numi tusuuna.

itukutu numi taakonin/tsaakuan.

r nAthair atá ar neamh,

o naofar d'ainm;

o dtaga do ríocht;

o ndéantar do thoil ar an talamh

mar a dhéantar ar neamh.

Ár n-arán laethúil tabhair dúinn inniu;

agus maith dúinn ár bhfiacha

mar a mhaithimidne dár bhféichiúna féin;

agus ná lig sinn i gcathú,

ach saor sinn ó olc.

Amen.

Irish

God, you our Fadda. You stay in da sky.

We like all da peopo know fo shua how you stay,

an dat you good an spesho inside,

an we like dem give you plenny respeck.

We like you come king ova hea now.

We like everybody make jalike you like, ova hea inside da world,

jalike da angel guys up inside da sky make jalike you like.

Give us da food we need fo every day.

Let us go, an throw out our shame fo all da kine bad stuff we do to you,

jalike us guys let da odda guys go awready,

an we no stay huhu wit dem fo all da kine bad stuff dey do to us.

No let us get chance fo do bad kine stuff,

But take us outa dea, so da Bad Guy no can hurt us.

[Cuz you our king, you get da real power,

an you stay awesome fo eva.]

Dass it!]

Hawaii Creole English (Pidgin)

Ein Tad yn y nefoedd,

sancteiddier dy enw;

deled dy deyrnas;

gwneler dy ewyllys,

ar y ddaear fel yn y nef.

Dyro inni heddiw ein bara beunyddiol,

a maddau inni ein troseddau,

fel yr ym ni wedi maddau i'r rhai a droseddodd yn ein herbyn;

a phaid â'n dwyn i brawf,

ond gwared ni rhag yr Un drwg.

Oherwydd eiddot ti yw'r deyrnas a'r gallu a'r gogoniant am byth.

Amen.

Welsh

First published in Great Britain
In 2005 by Scottish Christian Press
21 Young Street
Edinburgh
EH2 4HU

ISBN 190432519X

Typeset by Heather Macpherson

Printed and bound by Bookchase Ltd

Good News Bible
Scriptures quoted from the Good News Bible published by The Bible
Societies/ Harper Collins Publishers Ltd., UK, © American Bible Society,
1966, 1971, 1976, 1992.

INTRODUCTION

The Lord's Prayer holds a special place in our hearts as Jesus' specific teaching on how to pray:

"When you pray, do not use a lot of meaningless words, as the pagans do, who think that their gods will hear them because their prayers are long. Do not be like them. Your Father already knows what you need before you ask him. This then is how you should pray:

'Our Father in heaven
May your holy name be honoured;
May your Kingdom come;
May your will be done on earth as it is in heaven
Give us today the food we need.
Forgive us the wrongs we have done, as we forgive the wrongs that others have done to us.
Do not bring us to hard testing, but keep us safe from the Evil One.' "

(Matthew 6 v 7-13, GNB)

There has been and will continue to be much theological debate about these instructions, but here we have tried to show them in as simple a way as possible; to encourage children of all ages to explore the words afresh. Parents and carers may like to refer on to other Bible passages which explain more about God's love for us, with the aim of encouraging children to discuss and discover what God's love means for them as individuals.

"Let the little children come to me, and do not stop them, because the Kingdom of heaven belongs to such as these."

(Matthew 19 v 14)

OUR FATHER

As strong and as gentle

As Mummy and Daddy

The one who cares for us

Who never forgets us

Did you know the Bible
says that God is your
father and your mother?
This might sound strange,
but it's because God loves us
so much that we need never
feel lonely or afraid.

WHO ART IN HEAVEN
WHO IS IN HEAVEN

We can't see God

Yet He's always there

Close enough beside us

To hear every prayer

God is in heaven.
We can't move
between heaven and
earth, but God can.
We don't know
exactly where
heaven is, but we
do know that
everyone there is
happy. God is
love, and being
close to God
makes us
happy.

HALLOWED BE THY NAME

YOUR NAME IS HOLY

The one who made the mountains

Who put the colours in the sunset

This great and strong God

Is our own best friend

God's name is special - that's
what 'holy' and 'hallowed' mean.
Because of this we honour and
respect God, even though we can
call him our Father.

THY KINGDOM COME

YOUR KINGDOM COME

One day all the lying

All the stealing and the cheating

The sadness and the fighting

Will be gone for good

God's kingdom is a place where people don't fight or cheat or lie - it's a place where there is real love, which is a very powerful thing. It's also a place where people are happy.

THY WILL BE DONE ON EARTH
AS IT IS IN HEAVEN

YOUR WILL BE DONE, ON EARTH
AS IN HEAVEN

We need to ask God

What He really wants for us

Not for all the things

We'd just like ourselves

Jesus taught us to pray this prayer because he knew that God's will is the best thing for all of us. We need to understand that being selfish is not good for us, and that God wants the very best for each one of us.

GIVE US THIS DAY OUR DAILY BREAD

GIVE US TODAY OUR DAILY BREAD

Let us have enough, God

But not want too much

And let us have the love to share our plenty

With those who have so little

We can trust God to give us what we need, even to feed us and clothe us. When we trust God for these things, it is much easier to share what we have with anyone who needs it.

AND FORGIVE US OUR DEBTS

FORGIVE US OUR SINS

FORGIVE US OUR TRESPASSES

Often we do things

That make God sad

And sometimes we forget

The things we ought to do

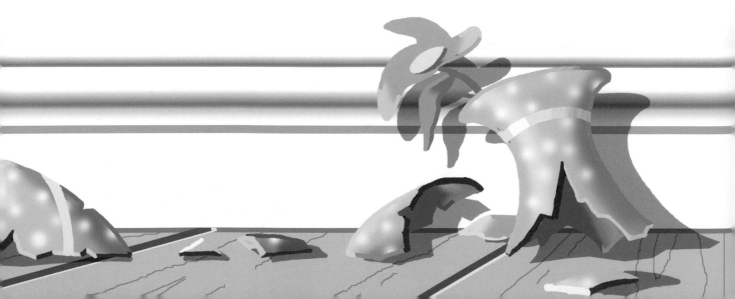

When you owe someone something it is called a debt. So we owe God if we do something wrong (this is called a sin or a trespass).

We can talk to God about it -

God is kind, he will forgive us.

AS WE FORGIVE OUR DEBTORS

AS WE FORGIVE THOSE WHO
SIN / TRESPASS AGAINST US

Just as God forgives us

For all that we do wrong

So we must forgive

All who're bad to us

God loves us so much
that he forgives us
willingly -

God wants us to
forgive others in
the same way.

AND LEAD US NOT INTO TEMPTATION

SAVE US FROM THE TIME OF TRIAL

We ask our loving God

That He will show us

The road that we should follow

And always be our guide

Sometimes life can be very difficult -
we ask God to protect us when this
happens. We ask God too to protect us
from going the wrong way and doing
things which are not good
for us.

AND DELIVER US FROM EVIL

We ask that God will hold us

In His strong hand

And keep us every day

From all wrong ways

We ask God to keep us safe
from all bad things.

FOR THINE IS THE KINGDOM,
THE POWER AND THE GLORY

FOR THE KINGDOM, THE POWER
AND THE GLORY ARE YOURS

Because He is our King

And loves us so much

This great Creator God

Who made everything good

God created everything and
it all belongs to him.
It's great to know he loves
us so much that he cares
about every hair
on our heads.

We agree!

So be it!

Amen!

Some people think that the language of Jesus' Prayer is old-fashioned and difficult to understand in today's world, so different from the world Jesus lived in. Martin Scott has written a new version of the prayer, which he hopes will help many more people to understand that God loves them and wants to care for them. Martin has tried to explain this in words which bring the images which Jesus used, like 'kingdom', into terms we might recognize more easily today. Jesus' words are still just as important today as they were then, and his Prayer is the best to way learn how to pray for ourselves and for our world.

God in heaven,

Your name is to be honoured.

May your new community of hope

be realised on earth as it is in heaven.

Give us today the essentials of life,

Release us from our wrongdoing

As we also release those who wrong us.

Do not test us beyond our means,

Save us from all that is evil;

For you embrace justice, love and peace,

Now and to the end of time, Amen.

Oor Faither in Heiven

Hallowt be Thy Name

Thy Kingdom come

Thy will be dune

On the Yird as in Heiven

Gie us oor breid for this incomin day

Forgie us the wrangs we hae wrocht, as we hae forgien the wrangs

we hae dree'd,

An say-us-na sairlie, but sauf us frae the ill-ane

An Thine be the kingdom, the Pooer an the Glory, noo an forivver.

Amen.

Scots Doric

Ar n-Athair a tha air nèamh,
Gu naomhaichear d'ainm.
Thigeadh do rìoghachd.
Dèanar do thoil air an talamh, mar a nithear air nèamh.
Tabhair dhuinn an-diugh ar n-aran làitheil.
Agus maith dhuinn ar fiachan,
amhail a mhaitheas sinne dar luchd-fiach.
Agus na leig ann am buaireadh sinn;
ach saor sinn o olc:
oir is leatsa an rìoghachd,
agus an cumhachd, agus a' ghlòir, gu siorraidh.
Amen.

Scots Gaelic

dad@hvn,
urspshl.
we want wot u want
&urth2b like hvn.
giv us food
&4giv r sins
lyk we 4giv uvaz.
don't test us!
save us!
bcos we kno ur boss
ur tuf
&ur cool 4 eva!
ok?

SMS English

Bapa kami yang ada di surga,
dimuliakanlah nama-Mu.
Datanglah kerajaan-Mu.
Jadilah kehendak-Mu
di atas bumi seperti di dalam surga.
Berilah kami rezeki pada hari ini,
dan ampunilah kesalahan kami,
seperti kami pun mengampuni
yang bersalah kepada kami.
Dan janganlah masukkan kami
ke dalam pencobaan,
tetapi bebaskanlah kami dari yang jahat.
Amin.

Indonesian

No
Qu
qu
qu
Do
pa
co
ne
ma
Ca
le
An

F

Taa Ahpu tomoba?atu,
U tekwapuha pitaruibe
Numi maaka ukiitsi tab
Nu tusuuna aiku numu
Keta aituku numi muhn
Taa Ahpu nansuwukai
Suni yutui o.

Comanche

Baba yetu uliye mbinguni,
jina lako litukuzwe.
Ufalme wako ufike.
Utakalo lifanyike duniani mbinguni.
Utupe leo mkate wetu wa kila siku.
Utusamehe makosa yetu,
kama tunavyowasamehe na sisi waliotukosea.
Usitutie katika kishawishi,
lakini utuopoe maovuni.
Amina.

Swahili

Pater Noster, qui es in caelis,
Sanctificetur nomen tuum.
Adveniat regnum tuum,
Fiat voluntas tua,
sicut in caelo, et in terra.
Panem nostrum quotidianum da nobis hodie,
Et dimitte nobis debita nostra,
sicut et nos dimittimus debitoribus nostris.
Et ne nos inducas in tentationem,
Sed libera nos a malo.
Amen.

Latin